Levers in Action

Gillian Gosman

PowerKiDS press.

New York

Published in 2011 by The Rosen Publishing Group, Inc.
29 East 21st Street, New York, NY 10010

First Edition

Editor: Maggie Murphy
Book Design: Kate Laczynski
Photo Researcher: Jessica Gerweck

Photo Credits: Cover, pp. 11 (bottom), 13,14, 16, 17, 18, 19, 22 Shutterstock.com; Back Cover and interior cement background graphic © www.iStockphoto.com/walrusmail; Back cover and interior graphic (behind some images) © www.iStockphoto.com/Ivan Gusev; p. 4 Bob Langrish/Getty Images; p. 5 Scott Boehm/Getty Images; p. 7 Erik Isakson/Getty Images; p. 8 © www.iStockphoto.com/DNY59; p. 9 © www.iStockphoto.com/Alejandro Rivera; p. 10 Ryan McVay/Getty Images; p. 11 (top) PhotoAlto/Odilon Dimier/Getty Images; p. 12 © www.iStockphoto.com/Lisa Turay; pp. 20, 21 © Rosen Publishing.

Library of Congress Cataloging-in-Publication Data

Gosman, Gillian.
  Levers in action / Gillian Gosman. — 1st ed.
    p. cm. — (Simple machines at work)
  Includes index.
  ISBN 978-1-4488-0682-9 (library binding) — ISBN 978-1-4488-1297-4 (pbk.) — ISBN 978-1-4488-1298-1 (6-pack)
  1. Levers—Juvenile literature. I. Title.
  TJ147.G68 2011
  621.8—dc22

                                        2009054346

Manufactured in the United States of America

CPSIA Compliance Information: Batch #216230PK: For Further Information contact Rosen Publishing, New York, New York at 1-800-237-9932

Contents

What Is a Lever?

A wheelbarrow is a kind of lever that helps you lift and move heavy loads. This girl is using a wheelbarrow to carry a heavy bale of hay.

Have you ever played on a seesaw at the playground? Have you ever pushed a wheelbarrow? Have you ever held a fishing pole or swung a baseball bat? If you have, you have used a lever! Each of these objects uses the help of **leverage** to raise or move a **load,** or weight.

The lever is one of six simple machines. These are all tools that help you do work. The **inclined** plane, the wheel and axle, the screw, the wedge, and the pulley are the other five simple machines. Each of these machines is simple, meaning it has few or no moving parts.

When you swing a baseball bat, you are using a lever. Levers are used in many other sports as well. Tennis rackets, golf clubs, field hockey sticks, and lacrosse sticks are all levers.

How Does a Lever Work?

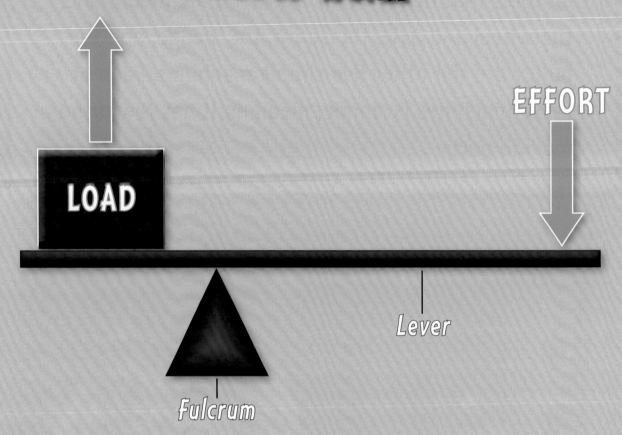

A lever is a long **plank**. The plank pivots, or turns, around a fixed point, called the **fulcrum**. Levers are often used to help lift or move heavy loads. Levers can also force an object away from another.

In order to lift a load, the force, or push or pull, applied to the load must be greater than the **resistance** of the load. Force is also called effort. A lever helps overcome, or beat, the resistance of the load because it multiplies the effort being applied to the load. This help is called the mechanical advantage of the machine. Levers are very **efficient** machines. This means that a lever does not waste the force you apply to it.

Different Kinds of Levers

A first-class lever, such as a hand truck, makes it possible to lift a heavy load with little effort.

There are three classes, or kinds, of levers. A lever is grouped into one of these classes based on the position of its fulcrum and direction of the effort applied to the lever.

The fulcrum of a first-class lever sits between the effort and the resistance. The effort is applied from above at one end of the plank. The fulcrum changes the direction of the force. The force applied to move one end of the plank down then drives the other end of the plank up. It is easier to lift a load if the end of the lever supporting the load is closer to the fulcrum than the end to which the effort is being applied. This is because the weight of the load is spread across the lever.

A crowbar, such as the one this man is using, is an example of a first-class lever. A crowbar can easily force two objects apart and remove nails from wood.

First-Class Levers at Work

These girls are playing on a seesaw made from two logs instead of a long plank and a metal bar. On this seesaw, the log on which the girls are sitting is the lever and the log beneath it is the fulcrum.

One example of a first-class lever is a playground seesaw. On a seesaw, the lever is the long plank on which children sit. The fulcrum is the metal bar at the middle of the plank on which the plank rests. The two children sitting on either end of the plank take turns applying resistance and effort. With the help of this lever, the effort of one child overcomes

When you use the claw end of a hammer to remove a nail from something, you are using the power of leverage to do the job more easily than you could using just your hands.

the resistance of the other child's weight and lifts her into the air.

The claw end of a hammer is another kind of first-class lever. When you use it to remove a nail from a wall, the nail is the load and the wall is the fulcrum. Two first-class levers joined at the fulcrum are called double levers. A pair of scissors is an example of a double lever.

A pair of chopsticks is an example of a double first-class lever. These people are eating their food with chopsticks.

Second- and Third-Class Levers

In a second-class lever, the load is placed between the fulcrum and the force. Here, the load is the pumpkins in the tray of the wheelbarrow.

In the case of a second-class lever, the fulcrum rests at one end of the plank. The effort is applied from below at the other end of the plank. The load is in the middle. A wheelbarrow is an example of a second-class lever. The wheel is the fulcrum, and the effort is applied by lifting the handles.

A third-class lever is one in which the fulcrum sits at one end of the plank, and the load sits at the other end. The effort is applied somewhere in between. Third-class levers are different from other levers because it takes more effort for a third-class lever to move a load. However, once effort is applied, third-class levers can make a load move quickly.

A tennis racket is an example of a third-class lever. When you apply effort to the racket by swinging it, the racket hits the tennis ball and makes it fly across the court.

The Earliest Levers

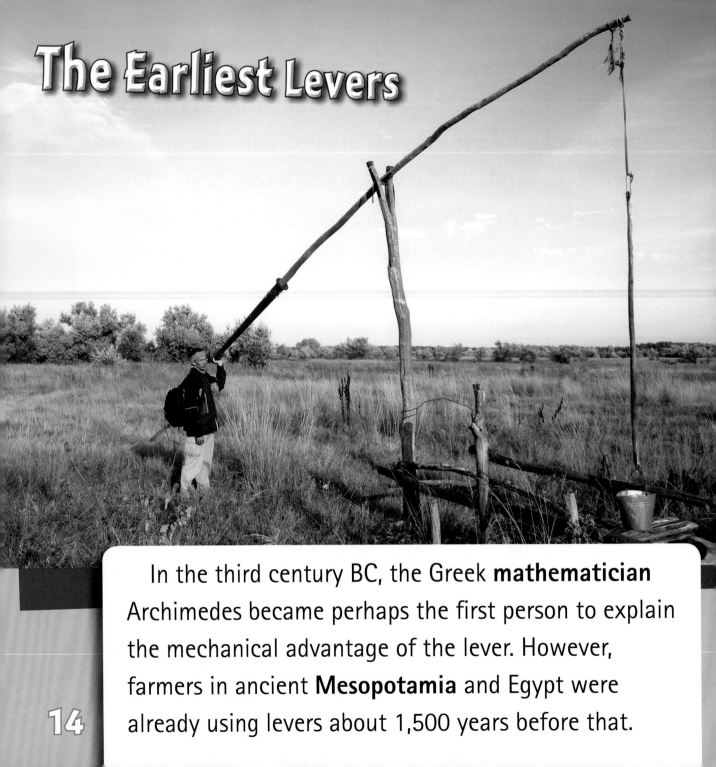

In the third century BC, the Greek **mathematician** Archimedes became perhaps the first person to explain the mechanical advantage of the lever. However, farmers in ancient **Mesopotamia** and Egypt were already using levers about 1,500 years before that.

These farmers built a machine called a shadoof to help them water their fields. The shadoof has a tall, wishbone-shaped fulcrum with a long pole laid across it. The fulcrum is much closer to one end of the pole than to the other. A bucket is hung from the long end of the pole. A clay weight is hung from the short end. The

The fulcrum of a shadoof sits between the effort and the load, making it a first-class lever. This man is using a shadoof to lift water from a deep well.

mechanical advantage of the pivoting pole makes it easy to dip the bucket into a river, fill it, then lift it up to water the ground. Some people in Asia and Africa still use these levers for lifting water today.

Levers Today

Today levers are used in heavy **industry**. One common industrial lever is the oil pump jack. This machine is used to lift oil out of wells dug deep into the ground.

In a pump jack, the force is made by a **motor**. The motor drives a beam, or long arm, up and down. The beam rests on a tall, A-shaped frame, which serves as the fulcrum. There is a weight

You can see pump jacks, such as these, in areas where oil is commonly found.

This is a tower crane, which is a kind of first-class lever. Workers use concrete blocks on one side of the crane to overcome the resistance of a heavy load hanging from the other side until the crane is balanced.

at one end of the beam. From the other end of the beam hangs a long **cable** that raises and lowers a metal **valve** deep under ground. The movement of the valve draws the liquid oil up the well.

Using Leverage Every Day

A nutcracker is a double second-class lever. The place where the two metal rods are joined together is the fulcrum, and the nut placed between them is the resistance.

Now we will take a closer look at a pair of scissors. Scissors are an example of a double lever you might use every day. You apply force to the levers by placing your fingers in the handle's openings and pulling them together. In doing so, you pull down on one lever and up on the other. The fulcrum changes the direction of the force you apply, bringing the blades of the scissors together. Whatever you are cutting, whether it is paper, cloth, or hair, serves as the load.

You might find some other levers, such as tweezers or a bottle opener, around your home. Can you find the fulcrum of the lever? Where would the load rest, and where would you apply the effort?

Scissors are really two first-class levers that share one fulcrum. The fulcrum in a pair of scissors is the screw that joins them in the middle.

An Experiment with Levers

In a first-class lever, the distance between the fulcrum and the load can be great or small. This distance helps decide how much effort is needed to lift the load. A simple **experiment** proves this.

What You Will Need:
- a broom
- a bag of books or blocks
- a friend

1. Stand with the broom resting over one shoulder and with its brush in front of you. Hold on to the broom tightly.

2. Ask your friend to hang the bag on the broom handle, which is behind you. Begin with

the bag near your shoulder, then ask your friend to slide the bag away from you and up the broom handle.

3. Does it become easier or harder to hold the load when the bag is moved away from your shoulder? Do you need to apply more or less effort to hold the load?

step 2

You Can Be a Lever, Too!

Picture the windup before a baseball pitcher throws the ball to the batter. The pitcher uses his ankles, knees, hips, shoulder, and wrist as fulcrums around which the effort of the pitch pivots.

His body acts as a lever, and the ball is the load.

The same is true when you swing a bat or a tennis racket. Your arm and the bat or racket come together as the lever's long plank. Your shoulder or elbow is the fulcrum, and the ball is the load. You are a living third-class lever!

Glossary

cable (KAY-bul) A heavy rope, often made of metal.

efficient (ih-FIH-shent) Working in the best possible way with the least waste of effort.

experiment (ik-SPER-uh-ment) A set of actions or steps taken to learn more about something.

fulcrum (FUL-krum) The point on which a lever pivots.

inclined (in-KLYND) Having a slope.

industry (IN-dus-tree) A business in which many people work and make money producing a product.

leverage (LEH-veh-rij) The added help of using a machine to do work.

load (LOHD) Something that must be carried or moved.

mathematician (math-muh-TIH-shun) A person who studies numbers.

Mesopotamia (mes-uh-puh-TAY-mee-uh) The ancient name for the land between the Tigris and Euphrates rivers.

motor (MOH-tur) A machine that makes motion.

plank (PLANGK) A long, flat piece of wood or metal.

resistance (rih-ZIS-tens) A force that works against another force.

valve (VALV) A tool that controls the flow of a liquid.

Index

Web Sites

Due to the changing nature of Internet links, PowerKids Press has developed an online list of Web sites related to the subject of this book. This site is updated regularly. Please use this link to access the list:

www.powerkidslinks.com/sm/lev/